Written by Marie-Pierre Klut
Illustrated by Luc Favreau

Specialist adviser:
Dr Susanna van Rose,
The Geological Museum, London

ISBN 1 85103 079 4
First published 1990 in the United Kingdom
by Moonlight Publishing Ltd
36 Stratford Road, London W8
Translated by Sue Birchenall

© *1987 by Editions Gallimard*
English text © *1990 by Moonlight Publishing Ltd*
Typeset in Great Britain by Saxon Printing Ltd, Derby
Printed in Italy by La Editoriale Libraria

POCKET • WORLDS

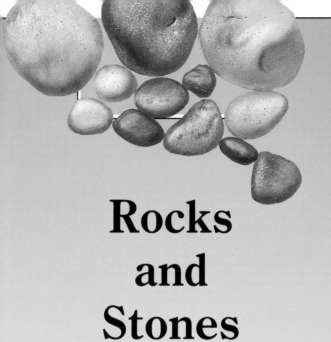

Rocks
and
Stones

Have you ever skimmed
a stone across the water?

Stones and rocks are everywhere, under your feet and all around you.

Houses are built of stone, and so are roads and pavements. In the country or on the beach, or in your garden, you can find pebbles of every shape and colour – you might even collect them.

Stone buildings provide shelter from heat and cold, rain and wind. Huge blocks of stone were hauled up, little by little, to build the Pyramids, which have survived the scorching sun of the Egyptian desert for almost 5,000 years.

Fossils are stones containing the remains of plants and animals that lived millions of years ago.

As hard as rock

Stones, or rocks, are made up of one or more minerals, bonded together into a hard, solid mass. Each mineral has a different chemical composition.

Rocks and minerals are not growing, living things, like plants and animals and people. But, in their own way, they too move and change.

Rocks give our world all its varied landscapes.

Cliffs falling sheer to the sea, the gentle slopes of ancient volcanoes, shifting sand-dunes in the desert, jagged peaks of bare rock that spear the sky . . . Earth movement, wind, frost, heat, and water have twisted, eroded, melted, or broken up the different types of rock.

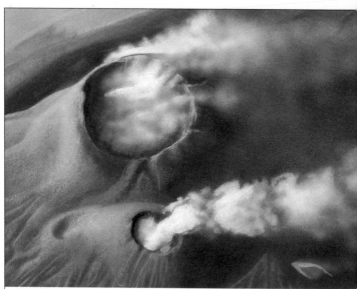

Smoke billows from the cones of an active volcano.

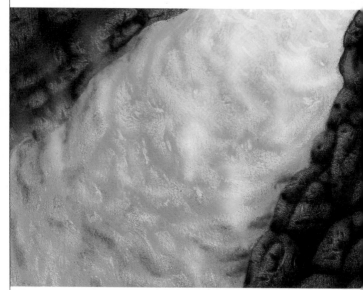

Liquid rock, called lava, streams from the crater like a river of fire, gradually cooling and hardening into volcanic rock.

Volcanic rock: obsidian, basalt, vesicular basalt

Different types of rock are formed in different ways. Burning-hot liquid rock, called magma, from deep within the Earth sometimes blasts its way out through a crack in the Earth's surface: a volcanic eruption. This type of rock is called **volcanic.**

Blocks of volcanic basalt form the Giant's Causeway, in Northern Ireland.

◄On the sides of the Grand Canyon, in Arizona, U.S.A., you can clearly see all the layers of limestone and red sandstone, stacked one on top of the other.

Other rocks are formed over millions of years, by the slow accumulation of debris – fragments of stone, bits of shell, animal bones . . . **These are sedimentary rocks**, from the Latin *sedere*, to sit down. Limestone, for example, is made up of pieces of coral, algae, and shells that drifted down to the sea-bed long, long ago.

Shellfish, like this nautilus, die and sink to the sea-bed . . .

Sometimes, at the foot of a waterfall, you can find leaves and plants preserved in limestone or tufa. Sandstone, another sedimentary rock, is formed from grains of sand compressed together by the weight of the rocks above.

. . . Millions of years later we find them as fossils, perfectly preserved in the sedimentary rock.

Underground palaces

In limestone country, spectacular caves are formed when rainwater seeps down through the rock and gradually washes away the layer of limestone. Water drips from the cave roof and splashes onto the floor below. Very, very slowly, over hundreds of years, the mineral salts in the water begin to form into stone icicles, some suspended from the roof, others growing up from the floor where the drips of water fall. Eventually those above, the **stalactites**, may reach down to meet the **stalagmites** on the ground, forming complete columns.

The mineral deposits take on all sorts of shapes – fluted pillars, squat mushrooms, spiky towers: a fairy-tale palace in the darkness underground.

Thick beds of leaves and stems lay matted together in the primeval swamps millions of years ago.

Gradually the plant remains turned into peat. You can burn peat on your fire, though it's very smoky.

Lignite is peat that has been compressed. It breaks up very easily.

Coal is formed when lignite is compressed even more tightly by the rocks around it. Coal blackens your fingers when you touch it.

Finally, the last stage: anthracite, the best coal of all. It burns well and gives off lots of heat.

How is coal formed?

Millions of years ago vast forests, and jungles of giant ferns, grew in swamps and shallow lagoons. As plants and trees died, they sank into the swamps. Gradually their remains were compressed under more and more layers of mud and rock, until all the water was squeezed out, leaving a hard, black substance: coal.

Men have mined coal since the Middle Ages, for heating and, nowadays, to generate electricity. Some coal is mined at the surface, in opencast mines, but most is found deep underground. Even with modern machinery, coal-mining is dirty, sometimes dangerous work.

During the Industrial Revolution, in the 18th and 19th centuries, many children worked down the mines.

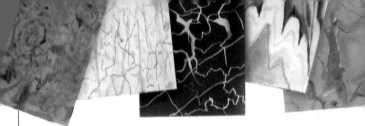

Since the days of the Ancient Greeks, people have prized the beauty of marble.

When mountains are formed by movements of the Earth's crust, the intense heat and pressure as the rocks are folded alters the form of the stone.

A marble quarry. The world's most famous marble comes from Carrara, in Italy, which supplied stone to Michelangelo.

Slate roofs are popular in mountain areas because they can withstand rain, snow, and high winds.

Rock changed in this way is called **metamorphic**, from the Greek words for change of form.

Marble is produced when limestone is subjected to high temperatures. It is easy to carve, and polishes up beautifully, so for centuries it has been used to build and decorate magnificent temples, churches, palaces, and stately homes. And many of the world's most famous sculptures have been carved from blocks of marble.

Slate is formed when mud is compressed very tightly. Because it splits easily into thin sheets, it is often used for roofing. Once upon a time schoolchildren wrote on slate with a piece of chalk, instead of using paper and pencil.

Why do you find sand and pebbles on the seashore?

Pebbles are lumps of stone that have been tossed about by the water. Their sharp edges disappear, and they become smooth and round.

Over the years they gradually wear away until they have become small pebbles, then gravel, and tiny grains of sand.

The sea erodes the cliff-base until the overhang collapses. In time the huge rocks are worn down to tiny pebbles.

Glaciers, too, grind rocks into gravel. In the desert, the extremes of heat and cold split the rocks, and the wind slowly erodes them down to sand.

Diamonds and other precious stones are found in rocks, sometimes deep underground.
People in different parts of the world search for them in all sorts of ways.

This huge crater has been excavated by people mining for diamonds.

These men sifting through the red soil are looking for diamonds too.

In Sri Lanka people use long-handled rakes to find precious stones in the gravel of the river-bed.

Bamboo scaffolding curves over this Indian mine.

Gem-hunters in Africa use long poles to lever up the boulders.

Jewels in the rocks

Most minerals form regular-shaped solids known as **crystals**. They range in size from microscopic to several metres long.

Pyrite

Fluorite

Rock-salt

Sparkling, brightly coloured, delicately shaped: many crystals are extremely beautiful.

Beryl comes in various colours. Long crystals like these are called prismatic, and may reach 8m in length.

This mineral group is rather like a bunch of grapes.

Crystals made up of fine needles, looking a bit like a porcupine.

The long, fine threads of asbestos crystals can be woven together to form cloth.

Because crystals are orderly patterns of atoms, they sometimes have several flat surfaces called faces.

A single mineral type may take many different forms:

Rock-crystal:
large, clear
quartz crystals

Quartzite:
grains of quartz
fused together

Obsidian:
quartz glass

Mohs' scale has been used to compare the hardness of different minerals since 1818.

The higher the number, the harder the mineral. The hardest is the diamond.

1 Talc

2 Gypsum

3 Calcite

4 Fluorite

5 Apatite

6 Orthoclase

7 Quartz

8 Topaz

9 Corundum

10 Diamond

Diamonds can be scratched only by other diamonds.

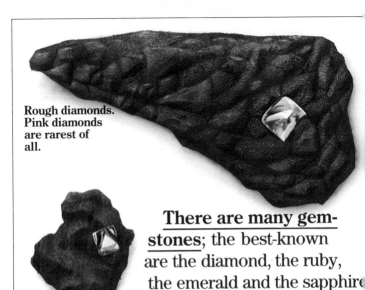

Rough diamonds.
Pink diamonds
are rarest of
all.

There are many gem-stones; the best-known are the diamond, the ruby, the emerald and the sapphire. All are rare and beautiful.

Diamonds come in lots of colours!

Precious stones are skilfully cut and polished to bring out all their colour and fire.

Ruby   Sapphire   Emerald

Other minerals can be gem-stones too.

The more transparent and clear they are, the greater their value.

Zircon **Tourmaline** **Garnet** **Topaz** **Amethyst**

Transparent stones sparkle brilliantly. Translucent stones have a softer, milkier look.

Agate **Chrysoprase** **Amazon-stone** **Amber**

Opaque stones are like beautiful pebbles; you can't see through them at all. The various shades of colour can produce delicate patterns.

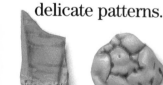

Lapis-lazuli **Turquoise** **Malachite** **Jade**

Nature's paintbox

The soil in your garden may look an unexciting brown, but soil and rocks produce a whole range of colours which have been used by artists throughout the centuries. Even in prehistoric times people knew how to make paints by crushing coloured rocks and mixing the powders with animal fats.

Prehistoric artists used a mixture of brown and green clays, chalk, and charcoal.

American Indians painted their faces in different ways according to the occasion: a battle, a buffalo-hunt, a celebration . . .

Malachite was first used in Egypt during the Bronze Age.

Realgar was also discovered by the Ancient Egyptians.

Medieval artists liked yellow orpiment because it looks like gold.

The ultramarine blue of lapis-lazuli came from Persia.

Powdered haematite, a warm reddish-brown, was also used as skin make-up.

The Great Wall of China is so long that it can be seen by astronauts in space. Each section is built with stone from the surrounding area, so the materials vary from place to place.

Stone for building

Because stone is heavy and difficult to move, houses and roads are usually built from rock found locally. The main types of stone used in building are limestone, granite, and sandstone.

The Taj Mahal, in India, is made entirely of marble.

Nowadays most buildings are constructed from bricks, tiles, and concrete, which are cheaper than natural stone. They too are made from minerals.

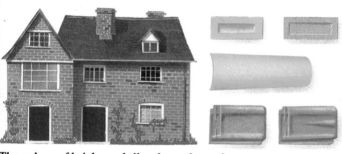

The colour of bricks and tiles depends on the type of clay they are made from.

Wet clay is easy to cut and shape into bricks and tiles, which are then fired in a kiln until they are hard. Concrete is the main material in most modern buildings. Its chief ingredient is cement, which is made by heating and crushing clay and limestone.

Concrete is a mixture of cement, sand, gravel, and water.

Scientists think that several meteorites found in Antarctica may have come from the Moon, because they are so similar to Moon-rocks collected by American astronauts.

Rocks from other worlds

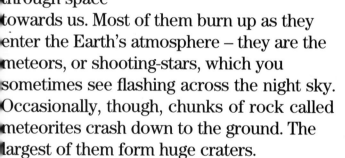

Sometimes rocks from planets millions of miles away come hurtling through space towards us. Most of them burn up as they enter the Earth's atmosphere – they are the meteors, or shooting-stars, which you sometimes see flashing across the night sky. Occasionally, though, chunks of rock called meteorites crash down to the ground. The largest of them form huge craters.

This vast crater was made by a meteorite with a diameter of one kilometre. Don't worry, though – meteorites this size hit the Earth's surface only once every ten thousand years!

People use minerals all the time.

Perhaps you wrote on the blackboard at school today. The chalk you used is made from the mineral gypsum.

To make gypsum into sticks of blackboard chalk, the rock is ground down to powder and then moulded into shape.

Or perhaps you sprinkled talcum powder over yourself after your bath. Talc is the softest mineral of all.

A pumice stone will get inkstains off your fingers. Pumice is solidified lava froth, and the only rock that floats.

Talc

A whetstone is used to sharpen knives, scissors and axes.

Neither animals nor people could survive without salt. Farmers put out blocks of it for their animals to lick.

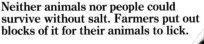

An eagle-stone is a hollow pebble with another stone inside, which jingles like a bell when you shake it. It is supposed to protect you from danger.

Some people believe that minerals have mysterious powers.

Australian aborigines believe the sky is a dome made of rock-crystal, which for them is a precious, magic stone.

Index

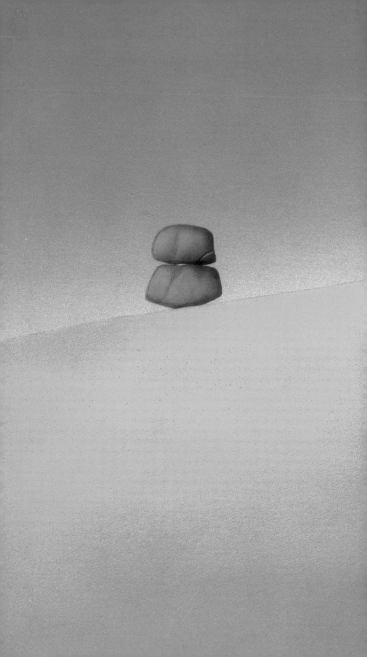